I0711680

TOP NUTRITION
TIPS
TOP NUTRITIONAL TIPS FOR A STRONGER,
HEALTHIER & HAPPIER YOU!
HEALTH
H₂O

Table of Contents

Introduction

Maintaining a healthy lifestyle doesn't take as much effort as you may think. Watching the habits of other healthy people, you might say to yourself, *"I could never do all of that."*

But that's just not true!

A person of optimal health leads a different daily routine than most people. Their lives are comprised of many, small, healthy habits that they continue to follow every day. These habits aren't complicated, and you are more than able to incorporate them into your own fitness and food planning.

In fact, living a healthy lifestyle can often simplify your life in ways you couldn't begin to understand. It takes a little bit of effort, some motivation, and a sincere want to change the way you live, move, and eat. If you have those attributes, replacing the old habits with the new will be simple.

This report is for anyone looking for easy ways to make their lives healthier and happier!

Let's look at some of the easiest ways that you can become a healthier person implementing these daily habits!

Important Note: It's important that you seek the advice and approval from your health care provider prior to making any drastic changes to your diet or exercise.

Tip #1: Consume Carbohydrates

Whenever you hear the word 'carbs,' chances are, your outlook is less than favorable. After all, just look at all those high protein/low carb diets.

What runs through your mind every time you see a plate of carbs? Breads, pastas, sugars, and starchy vegetables, right? All of things we've been told to stay as far away as possible from.

But surprise! **Our bodies actually need carbs.**

The problem isn't carbs, it's the **type of carbs** that we are consuming.

The ones we should be avoiding are found in white flours, processed sugars, and white rice.

The ones we should be consuming, however, are found in foods like oatmeal, whole grains, and brown rice. These types of carbs are called Complex Carbohydrates.

Here are some easy ways to incorporate complex carbohydrates into your daily diet.

- **Steel Cut Oats:** Steel cut oats are better for you than regular oats because they're not as heavily processed. The high fiber content makes them perfect candidate to eat away at bad cholesterol. Pick some up at your grocery store and have them for breakfast with a banana or avocado!

- **Quinoa:** If you're either allergic to gluten or just want to eliminate it from your diet, then consider adding quinoa to your list of complex carbohydrates. Not only are they high in fiber, but they have a good amount of protein, and even comes with some omega-three fatty acids. Talk about a superfood!

- **Lentils:** If you're a vegetarian and looking for more plant-based protein, or just looking to ease up on eating so much meat, then lentils are a must.

Not only are they also full of fiber, but they're loaded with cancer-fighting polyphenols and folic acid, which helps combat heart disease. Plus, there are so many ways to enjoy this tasty legume. Just search the internet for some recipe ideas!

So, the next time you hear someone put down carbs, remind yourself-and them-about the importance of complex carbohydrates!

Tip #2: Portion Control

Have you ever heard the saying, "Your eyes are bigger than your stomach?"

It's easy to overestimate how much food you really need to consume in order to feel full and satisfied, which is why it's important to go out of your way to monitor your portion sizes.

Before you grab a plate, remember that quality is more important than quantity.

Pay attention to what you're about to consume, not how much. Just because you're eating a salad, doesn't mean its necessarily good for you. Dressings can contain simple sugars, chemicals, and heavy fat content.

In reality, eating too much of anything is bound to make you feel bad, regardless of how good it tastes. Just think about the last time you ate a few too many slices of pizza!

Here are some tips for you when you're creating your meals.

Portion Size of Meat: A grilled or broiled chicken breast, lightly seasoned, is a great source of lean protein. But it should be about the size of your palm, roughly 6-8 ounces.

You can also purchase a food scale to weigh your food before or after cooking for a more precise measurement. If it's too big, trim some off and save it for your next meal!

Ease Up on The Pasta: Most people would probably agree that pasta is delicious, but a serving is actually about the size of your fist. That doesn't seem like much.

Remember that pasta tends to fill you up very quickly. Have you ever felt bloated after eating too much spaghetti? Then you probably ate more than a fistful!

Invest in Smaller Dinnerware: You know those small plates that come with dinnerware sets, the ones that are supposed to be used for snacks?

Well, they can actually make great dinner plates!

Depending upon how small yours are, try using one of those for your next meal and take note of your level of satisfaction compared to eating off the larger plate.

Mentally, your brain sees a full plate, and though it isn't as much food as the other plate, you are getting your fill and then stopping. With the larger plate, you would have continued until you had eaten too much.

Just remember that size matters when it comes to what you're eating. Even if something is good for you, such as grilled chicken or a lean burger, you can still have too much of it!

Tip #3: Celebrate Small Victories

Not a single person out there goes from unhealthy to perfectly fit, with all positive habits, overnight. It's not possible. What is possible is creating **small changes that lead to small victories.**

Those small victories will eventually graduate into larger ones.

The decision to commit to a healthy lifestyle is a huge undertaking.

First off, you should start your new journey off with a celebration. Get excited about taking the first big step toward a better and healthier you.

Next, make sure you are realistic with yourself and know that there will be times that you will have to force yourself to get up, to eat healthy, and sometimes it can be a real struggle.

It won't last forever.

With time and commitment, your goals will slowly come closer into focus.

The best way to keep yourself motivated is to celebrate every small victory along the way.

No matter how small something is, you should always take time to congratulate yourself for working so hard!

Here are a few of those milestones you should be celebrating.

Working Out Five Days in One Week: If you're going from a sedentary lifestyle to an active one, then you're in for a major change, possible shock. It's not easy giving up those nights on the couch, scrolling through your phone while binge-watching your favorite shows.

But when you make the sacrifice and give up some of that time to work out, and do it for a full five days, then you should celebrate your achievements!

Losing Just One Pound: If you have a significant amount of weight to lose, it can seem like an uphill battle that can't be won. But guess what? It absolutely can be won!

Remember that when you step on the scale and it only goes down by one number, because it's bound to happen eventually.

The truth is, even one pound is an accomplishment. To compare it to something you can visualize, one pound of fat is the same volume as a pound of butter. Not too shabby!

Better Quality of Life: It's common for those of us who are overweight to easily become out of breath doing every day simple activities.

Walking, climbing the stairs, even talking too quickly can turn into a case of heavy breathing. With daily exercise and more nutritional foods, your cardiovascular system will begin to heal, and if you're paying attention, it doesn't take forever.

When you finally finish that 60-minute workout without stopping, and your heartrate and breathing is at a normal high intensity level, it's time to celebrate.

Tip #4: Map Out Your Game Plan

You wouldn't go on a trip without a map, be it a paper one or a GPS device, so why would you commit to a healthier lifestyle without a plan?

Just like you make up a shopping list before heading to the grocery store, you should also map out the path to your goal.

It's just not feasible to go about an overhaul of your life without a game plan. What are you going to eat?

What exercise program will you follow? What will you be giving up in search of a healthier you?

There are so many things to consider before beginning your journey, and mapping it all out is a great way to organize your thoughts.

Remember that failure to plan is planning to fail, and you want this new lifestyle to be a success!

Here are a few ways to map out your success.

Establish A Daily Schedule: The days go by quickly, and it's easy to get sucked into doing something other than what you wanted to do.

Write down a schedule for each day of the week and incorporate the times you'll be exercising, meal prepping, and so forth.

Do your best to stick to that schedule. Say goodbye to unproductive days!

Exercise Goals: If your goal is to run a marathon, then you need to first know how far you can currently run, and then work your way up in increments to reach your ultimate goal.

Push yourself a little bit more each week until you have reached and sustained your goal! Even then, why not start all over with a brand-new goal?

Dietary Needs: Never leave what you're going to eat up to chance. Plan your meals out ahead of time, for the entire week if possible.

When you've planned it out, you won't fall victim to fast food, takeout, or other quick temptations. And don't forget to incorporate healthy snacks!

Tip #5: Hydrate

Water may not taste as good as sugary soda, but our bodies depend on it. In fact, our body is comprised of about 60% water. That's more than half!

As we go about our day, we continuously lose that precious water through our pores. This is why we need to keep hydrating.

Soda and other sugary drinks dehydrate us, so commit to gulping more H2O each and every day!

If you're worried that you'll have to sip it out of a boring mug or glass, don't worry. Thanks to the internet, there's more than one way to fill up! But in reality, there's no reason to spend money on fancy bottles and gadgets. A simple cup and tap will suffice.

Keep reading for tips on how to stay hydrated!

Here are some ways to make sure you are consistently getting your recommended daily servings of water.

Bring Two Liters with You to Work: If you prefer the refreshing taste of a bottled water, then consider buying several liters for the week. Every night before you go to bed, make sure you have two refrigerated, and put them in a cooler next to an ice pack in the morning. Off to work you go with your daily water!

Purchase A Fun Bottle: You can now purchase refillable water bottles that have inspiring quotes, such as "you're doing great," and "keep going." These messages can be inspirational, funny, or motivating, it really doesn't matter.

What does matter, is getting every lost drop. It's an easy and fun way to keep your body hydrated!

Tip #6: Stock Your Refrigerator

Is there anything worse than a growling stomach with nothing ready and prepared?

This is one of the most common ways that you can accidently thwart your own road map to success. It is far too easy to jump online and order take out. You should always keep your kitchen stocked with nutritious food!

You don't need a large amount of food to be able to whip up some quick meals. (Remember Chapter 2 where we discussed limiting your portion sizes.)

All it takes is a basic protein source, a mixture of fresh and frozen veggies, and simple cooking skills. Voila! A hearty, healthy meal is never more than a few minutes away.

Be specific with the items you purchase form the grocery store. Quick and easy does not have to be terrible for you.

Here are some of the food items you should always have on hand.

Lean Protein: Chicken, 90/10 beef, lentils, beans, low glycemic fruit, and nuts. Just make sure, if you don't have time to soak and cook your beans, go for the low sodium canned variety. It's better to make it work with your schedule then to abandon it altogether.

When choosing nuts, go with a lower fat nut like almonds. They are filling, tasty, and keep forever.!

Frozen Vegetables: Frozen vegetables last longer than fresh ones. Make sure to always have a few bags stored away in your freezer, such as mixed, broccoli, kale, peas, and carrots. There are plenty to choose from at your local supermarket and they can be ready within minutes!

Salad Kits: A good, hearty salad is often what's needed after a long day. Add in some lean protein and maybe even a side of prepared frozen veggies, and you have yourself a delicious, healthy salad in just a few minutes!

If you're wondering about dressing, a simple vinegar and oil is easy, quick, and usually stocked in most kitchens.

Tip #7: Prepared Meals

Sometimes we just don't have time to whip up even a quick meal, but our stomach is telling us that it's time to refuel. On these days, it's great to be able to purchase a prepared meal at your local grocery store.

Due to the rise of consciousness in physical health and wellness, supermarkets have started to catch on and are stocking their prepared foods section with healthy alternatives.

So, while food to go may make you think of pizza, it's time you gave your local grocery store another look!

Remember that eating out can be expensive, but when your alternative is just as pricey junk food, know you're putting your money to good use. Your body will thank you for it later. Sometimes life just gets in the way.

Keep reading for suggestions on buying pre-made food!

High Protein Meals: As tempting as that spaghetti-to-go dish may look, try and steer clear of pasta and sugary sauces, and instead, go for the chicken breast and veggies. Stores will often season their meats too, so don't worry about a lack of flavor!

Protein Shakes: If plans are going to keep you on the road for a while, then look for a protein shake that you can either fix on the go, or is pre-packaged.

Many health food stores make protein shakes in-house and keep them in the prepared foods section. Not only are these shakes nutritious, but they're also pretty tasty.

Prepared Snacks: You meant to prepare your snacks for the week, but something came up, so now what? Are you stuck hitting up the vending machine for a sugary candy bar? Not so fast! Take a few minutes and swing by your local grocery store where you're bound to find lots of healthy, prepackaged snacks like nuts, string cheese, and protein bites!

Tip #8: Zip-Lock Bags

There's never an excuse to not bring a healthy, pre-planned snack thanks to Zip-Lock bags. Not only do they come in a variety of sizes, but many of them allow you to write on the outside of the packaging, which makes meal prep even easier!

When you're stocking up on good food at the store, make sure to swing by the section that carries foil and plastic wrap. You'll find a large selection of Zip-Lock bags that are perfect for portioning out your snacks!

With these on hand, both at your job and at home, you can say goodbye to inhaling bags of potato chips, and hello to healthy, portioned out snacks. They're easy to stack in your cupboard, fit nicely in a lunch pail, and can even go in your purse.

Consider bagging peanuts, cashews, homemade granola bars, protein cookies, and other tasty healthy snacks. And be sure to look for new ideas and recipes online.

People around the world are uploading their own versions of healthy snacks on a daily basis.

Are you eco-friendly? Don't worry, companies like Clear Bags make Eco Friendly Compostable sandwich bags. And if you want something easier on your wallet, reusable zip bags can be found on Amazon.

Tip #9: A Healthy Dose of Pro-Biotics

Intestinal health is just as important as physical health. We consume both good and bad bacteria in the foods that we eat, and it's important to keep it all balanced.

One of the side effects of a buildup of bad bacteria is gastroenteritis. This can cause nausea, vomiting, diarrhea, and in extreme cases, hospitalization due to dehydration. Probiotics can both cure and prevent this nasty infection.

There are many ways to take probiotics nowadays, too.

The most common form is yogurt. Many people choose this option to get their daily dose of probiotics because of the taste, and because it's considered to be a healthy snack.

If you're not into the taste and texture of yogurt, however, you can also go with a supplement. There are many different brands on the market to choose from.

And in addition to yogurt and capsuled probiotic, there are now liquid versions of it too. Check your local grocery or health food store and see what probiotic drinks they have to offer.

Whatever method you choose to use, the end result will be a healthy gut full of good bacteria!

Tip #10: Daily Cardio

The research has been done, and the results have been out for quite some time: cardiovascular workouts are imperative to a long, healthy life.

Whether it's a daily walk or intense run on the treadmill, there are so many benefits to getting your heart rate up!

Working out your heart with cardiovascular exercise makes that beating all the stronger. When your heart is strong, it doesn't have to work so hard to pump, adding years to your ticker.

By keeping it in tip-top shape, it helps lower your chances of heart disease and diabetes. Both of which are life threatening and far too common in our society.

By committing to a daily cardio workout, be it big or small, you can lower your chances of those, and many other illnesses. Talk about a small change with a big, long-lasting impact!

Consider doing either a thirty-minute cardio session each day, or several that add up to thirty minutes.

And of course, check with your doctor first to make sure you're healthy enough to take on this amount of exercise. And don't forget your rest days. Even with a goal in mind, you want to give your body time to rejuvenate and heal.

Resources

Here are links to a few resources that I believe will help you:

Healthy Lifestyle Tips

>>https://www.eatthis.com/personal-trainer-tips/

Eat This is a great website that shows you how easy it is to make small changes.

Food Hacks

>>https://www.onemedical.com/blog/eat-well/12-nutritional-hacks

One Medical knows that people like to enjoy what they're eating, and this is a great site to keep you on track.

Nutrition Tips

https://www.healthline.com/nutrition/27-health-and-nutrition-tips#section6

Health Line is a website that has lots of tips to keep your nutrition

at the top of its game.

www.ingramcontent.com/pod-product-compliance
Lightning Source LLC
Chambersburg PA
CBHW050710250726
48662CB00002B/945